Henny Croes

An excerpt from *Teach Us to Number Our Days*

A HEART *of* WISDOM

REFLECTIONS ON MATURITY

D0889463

An excerpt from *Teach Us to Number Our Days*

A HEART *of* WISDOM

REFLECTIONS ON MATURITY

DAVID ROPER

DISCOVERY HOUSE
PUBLISHERS

These excerpts from *Teach Us to Number Our Days*
© 2008 by David Roper
All rights reserved.

Requests for permission to quote from this book
should be directed to:
Permissions Department, Discovery House Publishers,
P.O. Box 3566, Grand Rapids, MI 49501.

Unless otherwise indicated, Scripture quotations are from the
New International Version®. ©1973, 1978, 1984 by
International Bible Society. Used by permission of Zondervan.
All rights reserved.

Cover Design: Stan Myers
Interior Design: Steve Gier

Printed in the United States of America

10 11 12 13 / DP / 5 4 3 2 1

Contents

Teach us to number our days aright,
that we may gain a heart of wisdom.

PSALM 90:12

BOOKS, NOTE CARDS, MEMOS, SHREDS AND SHARDS

*Books, note cards, memos, shreds and shards of some
fresh-excavated pile or file; an hour on this, an hour on that.*

—T. M. MOORE

S ome years ago I came across William Penn's classic work, *Some Fruits of Retirement.* He wrote in his introduction: "He [Penn] has now had some Time he could call his own; a Property he was never so much Master of before." Having retired from public life, Penn now had more time to report his thoughts on his final years.

Although I'm not retired, my schedule is relaxed these days, and I have more time to call my own—time for reading, reflection, and prayer. These essays are, in part, the fruit of that "retirement."

This collection is eclectic in nature, based on things I've seen, experienced, read, or thought about in recent years. They're made up of "memos, shreds and shards" drawn from my journals, letters, e-mails, and a host of jottings that I've sent out to a few friends from time to time.

I write from the perspective of an older person, having crossed the biblical boundary of "three-score and ten years" five years ago. Though more or less "hale and hearty," as they say of old timers, I know I'm living on borrowed time. With Cowper, I want to "close life wisely and not waste my own." I suppose that's why I now feel compelled to pass on these scraps of writing, accompanied by Israel's old-timer's prayer: "Do not forsake me, O God, when I'm old and gray, *until I declare your power to the next generation*, your might to those who are to come" (see Psalm 71:18).

Yet this is not a book about aging, per se, though I do cover many of the concerns that inhere as we grow older. More than anything else, it's about my own journey toward maturity. In that sense, though in my dotage, I'm still "coming of age."

As I read through these chapters again, in preparation for writing this introduction, it also occurred to me that almost all of them have something to do with the goodness of God. That's to be expected, I suppose, for through the years I truly have "tasted the kindness of the Lord" (1 Peter 2:3 NASB).

Our culture is constantly telling us, in one way or another, that youth is the time of "wine and roses," but I must disagree. Despite the troubles of old age, and they are many, I must say, with the wedding guests at Cana, that my Lord has saved the best wine for the last. He has touched these final years of my life with delightful sweetness, fragrance and bouquet. With Browning, "Let me attest . . . I have lived, seen God's hand through a lifetime, and all was for the best!"

David Roper
Boise, Idaho

FORGETFULNESS

If, on leaving the company, a young man cannot
remember where he has left his hat, it is nothing.
But when an old man forgets, everyone says,
"Ah, his memory is going."

—DR. SAMUEL JOHNSON

L ately I find myself forgetting ordinary things on a regular basis. My misfortune manifests itself in a fading recollection of where I left my car keys, my reading glasses, my sunglasses, my hat.

I even forget my best thoughts, which seem to come and go at random; I have little control over them these days. Plato said our minds are like aviaries and our thoughts are like birds. It's an apt metaphor for me. I reach for one thought and frighten it away, then grasp at another that quickly flits away from my mind—unless I write it down.

There are other things I've forgotten, but right now I can't remember what they are.

There's an upside to forgetting, however. There are things I *want* to forget, not the least of which are the things in the past that I could have, should have, done. John Greenleaf Whittier said, "Of all sad words of tongue or pen, the saddest are these: 'It might have been.'" Indeed.

I think of relationships I might have nurtured, projects I should have finished, decisions that were better unmade. And certainly my past behavior has been regrettable. An old acquaintance recently characterized me as "a mean kid" in my youth. It saddens me to think that he remembers me that way. I think of all the things I've "done, and been; the shame / Of motives late revealed, and the awareness / Of things ill done and done to others' harm" (T. S. Eliot). I wish I could forget them.

Further, I want to forget the wrongs I've received in my lifetime. It's easy to brood over them and become bitter and resentful, like Charles Dickens's sad, eccentric Miss Havisham, who was jilted at the altar and stopped all the clocks in her house at the hour of her disappointment. Her bitterness was frozen in time. I don't want mine to be.

All of us, I'm sure, have been wronged in some way or another at various times; friends and enemies have dishonored and grieved us. We may cling to bitterness over our childhood and remember old wounds from a parent's hand.

Some rise above it and leave it behind. I once asked a cruelly abused friend how he dealt with his grievances. "I've got a good forgetter," he replied. I wish I could get one too.

All of which encourages me to recall the patriarch Joseph. He, too, had much to forget. He was "a mean kid" too, flaunting his most–favored status, wearing it on his sleeve, so to speak. (Joseph's "coat of many colors" was actually a long-sleeved garment with stripes on the sleeves to indicate rank. He wore it to parade his importance.)

Joseph further alienated himself from his family by endlessly relating his dreams—dreams that were true, as it turned out, but which, when repeated over and over, augmented the resentment of his brothers. They "hated him all the more because of his dreams and what he said" (Genesis 37:8). Israel's wise men would have called him a *peti*—a young fool.

In his youth, a series of calamitous events cascaded down on Joseph's head, like bricks tumbling out of a dump truck, one after another. He was snatched from his doting father by his brothers, cast into a pit, and passed on to a band of Bedouins who in turn sold him into slavery in Egypt.

In Egypt his life continued to be a series of tragic indignities. He was tempted by a determined seductress who, when spurned, accused him of raping her. He was summarily tried, convicted, imprisoned, and left to languish in isolation for a dozen years or more, forgotten by family and friends.

Yet in the end Joseph's bitterness was transformed into forgiveness and love. He named his firstborn son Manasseh (Hebrew for "caused to forget") for, he said, "God has made me forget all my trouble" (Genesis 41:51).

How did God cause him to forget? Did he work some magic on Joseph that erased his memory? No, God taught him to look at his past in a redemptive way: Joseph came to see that God's hand controlled all that he bore. And he knew that God's ways were "perfect" (Psalm 18:30).

Two texts underscore that perception: "You *sold* me," Joseph said to his brothers, "but God *sent* me here to preserve life." And again, "You *intended* to harm me, but God *intended* it for good to accomplish what is now being done, the saving of many lives" (see Genesis 45:5; 50:20, emphasis added).

Joseph remembered well what his brothers had done: they had sold him into slavery. That injustice and cruelty he could never forget. But behind the bitter experiences of the past he saw the providence of God. This is the mystery of sovereignty: God works through evil to accomplish His will. "He permits evil," Augustine said, "to transform it into good."

The past cannot be changed, but it can be redeemed. It cannot be forgotten *per se* (for some things will never be forgotten), but it can be swallowed up in God's sovereign purposes and left behind.

How can we forget the bitterness of our past? By seeing God's providence in every event of our lives, even in our mistakes and in others' malice. The God of love and wisdom has taken the worst that we have done and is turning it into eternal good. We may not see or know that good until we step into eternity itself, but it is certain—as certain as the lovingkindness of God.

MY STAFF

I'm growing fonder of my staff;
I'm growing dimmer in the eyes;
I'm growing fainter in my laugh;
I'm growing deeper in my sighs;
I'm growing careless of my dress;
I'm growing frugal of my gold;
I'm growing wise; I'm growing—yes—
I'm growing old.

—JOHN GODFREY SAXE

There's an antique rack in the entrance to our home in which we keep the canes and walking sticks of several generations of our family. My favorite is a slender staff with a gold–plated knob, engraved with the initials "DHR." It belonged to Carolyn's great-grandfather, whose name was Daniel Henry Rankin. Curiously, my initials are the same.

My study houses another stick collection: my father's peeled, apple-wood walking stick and an ancient, gnarled, blackthorn shillelagh among others.

Outside in a barrel in our garage there's an assortment of cross-country ski poles, wading wands, and trekking sticks I've gathered over the years. One of these days, I'll probably trade them all in for handrails and a walker.

I think of old Jacob, worshiping and "leaning on his staff" (see

Hebrews 11:21). Like Jacob, I too am crippled, broken-down, and ruined. I'll always need something or someone to lean on.

These days, when I set out on an enterprise that seems daunting for me at my age, I take this staff along with me: "The LORD will go before [me]" (Isaiah 52:12).

When I see my friends struggling with sin and guilt, I hold up this rod: May they "have power . . . to grasp how wide and long and high and deep is the love of Christ, and to know this love that surpasses knowledge" (Ephesians 3:18–19).

When there seems to be no time for reflection and quiet waiting and I think I must act *now,* I remember this stay: "Be still, and know that I am God" (Psalm 46:10).

When I note that my legs and heart have grown weaker and I can no longer wade swift streams, climb steep trails, and surmount other difficulties, I strengthen my inner person with this thought: God will not cast me away when I am old; He will not forsake me when my strength is gone. My strength now is in "quietness and confidence" (Isaiah 32:17).

When I think of death and its certainty, I remember God's faithfulness throughout my years: He has supported me with His right hand; He has guided me with His counsel; and "afterward [he] will take me into glory" (Psalm 73:24).

These truths and others are "the very staff of my age, my very prop" (William Shakespeare).

Old Jacob, weary and worn-out—once strong, but now humbled and utterly dependent on God—worshiped, leaning on the top of his staff. Like Jacob, I'm growing old and fond of my staff. I aim to keep it close at hand.

> *Lord*
> *With a crooked stick for a cane*
> *I'm limping home.*

Mocked and maligned
Stooped and stupid
Soiled and shabby
I limp toward You.

—RUTH HARMS CALKIN

AN AFTERTHOUGHT...

I re-read John Bunyan's *The Pilgrim's Progress* the other day and came across this passage:

> After this, Mr. Ready-to-halt called for his fellow-pilgrims, and told them, saying, I am sent for, and God shall surely visit you also. So he desired Mr. Valiant to make his will. And because he had nothing to bequeath to them that should survive him but his crutches, and his good wishes, therefore thus he said: These crutches I bequeath to my son that shall tread in my steps, with a hundred warm wishes that he may prove better than I have been.
>
> My staffs and crutches I bequeath to our three sons.

NO NEED
FOR REGRET

Remember not the sins of my youth
and my rebellious ways.

—PSALM 25:7

I f only I could live my life over again," we say, "I would do better."
Not likely. A fresh start for any of us would amount to almost nothing without the experience necessary to make the right adjustments.
"The light which experience gives us is a lantern on the stern, which shines only on the waves behind us," Coleridge said. Lacking the knowledge and understanding we've gained through the years, we'd make the same mistakes again.

I came across a poem by poet Hezekiah Butterworth one day that frightened me a good deal:

> *I walked through the woodland meadows,*
> *Where sweet the thrushes sing;*
> *And I found on a bed of mosses*
> *A bird with a broken wing.*
> *I healed its wound, and each morning*
> *It sang its old sweet strain;*
> *But the bird with a broken pinion*
> *Never soared as high again.*

I found a young life broken
By sin's seductive art
And touched with a Christlike pity,
I took him to my heart.
He lived with a noble purpose,
And struggled not in vain;
But the life that sin had stricken
Never soared as high again.

I said to myself, "Is it true? Have my sins irreparably stricken and crippled me? Can I never soar as high again?"

Indeed we can—all of us—for God does *not* remember the sins of our youth. Love has paid the price, and thus our most outrageous and oft-repeated sins have been forgiven according to God's mercy and grace. We cannot drift beyond His love and care. Beyond the bad news of our failure is the good news of grace—the stupendous free gift of God.

Grace means that God forgives us, no matter what we have done, are doing, or will ever do again. It means that our sins are gone forever —replaced by Love.

Our Lord gives us this assurance: "Whoever comes to me I will *never* drive away" (John 6:37, emphasis added). He freely pardons; He abundantly forgives (Isaiah 55:7; Psalm 130:3–4). We will be welcomed, no matter what we have done, if only we will come to Him.

Grace also means that God has given us the resources to make a new beginning. The question is not, "Can I make it? Am I able? Can I overcome my habitual sin?" The question is, "Is *He* able?" Can *He* transform me?" He says He can, though it may take awhile. Love perfects that which it begins. He will not forsake the work of His hands (see Psalm 138:8).

We must start with God's part, with the calm assurance that grace for the next act of obedience is already there. We don't have to worry about tomorrow, or this afternoon; we can move forward without fear or frustration knowing that the next step will take care of itself. That's the comfort we need to give to ourselves.

Furthermore, we must know that God's love will *continue* to cover our sins, no matter what we do. God is never disappointed—nor is He surprised—by human failure, for it is inevitable. "It is a consoling idea," wrote Danish philosopher Søren Kierkegaard, "that we are *always* in the wrong."

Long ago God made provision for our evil. Before we were born, before we did anything good or bad, Jesus paid for *all* our sins—those that were, those that are, and those that shall be. Now, despite false starts and failures, God is at work conforming some small part of us to His likeness, making us His portrait, His reproduction, His work of fine art. We can be confident of this: "He who began a good work in [us] will carry it on to completion" (Philippians 1:6).

God is never in a hurry, but He does mean business. He will finish the work as soon as He can.

"But" we say, "I have wasted so much of my life. Can I still be of use?" God wastes nothing, not even our sins. When acknowledged, they humble us and make us more merciful to others in their weakness. We can become more approachable, more useful to God and to others. Indeed, each loss has its own compensation.

And there is more: Sin can make us more appreciative of God's forgiveness and can lead us to a deeper, more extravagant love for Him than we could otherwise attain. Once we know how much we've been forgiven, we love Him all the more (see Luke 7:47). Thus "broken pinions" heal fully and we **can** fly.

Another poet has amended Butterworth's lines:

> *The soul that comes to Jesus*
> *Is cleansed from every stain;*
> *And by grace that is freely given,*
> *We **can** soar higher again.*

IN THIS PLACE

Being born is the front end of our troubles.

—MISTER ROGERS

As a young man I was led to believe that the end of life would be easier than its beginning, but as I've aged I've come to the conclusion that some of the hardest tests are farther along.

Take Abraham, for example. After enduring a lifetime of difficulty, the old patriarch finally retired to a life of ease and affluence near the wells of Beersheba. He and Sarah enjoyed good old age with Isaac, their love and laughter. They were in their "golden years."

One night Abraham put his head on his pillow, thanked God for His goodness, and went to sleep, only to be jolted awake in the middle of the night by a voice beckoning him. "Abraham!"

"Here I am," Abraham replied.

"Take your son, your only son, Isaac, whom you love, and go to the region of Moriah. Sacrifice him there as a burnt offering on one of the mountains I will tell you about"(Genesis 22:1–2).

Isaac was the son of Abraham's old age, the promised child through whom God pledged to make him great. Abraham knew that the gods of the Chaldeans and Canaanites demanded human sacrifice. Was his God now demanding this of him? Why?

Indeed, we ask when life is sweet and then turns bitter, "Why?"

Did Abraham tell Sarah? I don't know. The ancient rabbis thought so, and said that Sarah held Isaac all that night, and that the ordeal contributed to her death. (Sarah's death came soon after: see Genesis 23:1–2.) But, for myself, I think Abraham told no one. This was a matter he had to work out with God alone.

Early the next morning Abraham packed up and started his terrible journey to Mount Moriah. There, the two—Abraham and his son—began their ascent to "the place" that God had revealed (see Genesis 22:3–19).

Isaac turned to his father and spoke: "Father, the fire and wood are here, but where is the lamb for the burnt offering?" Abraham replied, "God himself will provide." With those words he rested his case.

You know the story: "Abraham looked up and there in a thicket he saw a ram caught by its horns. He . . . took the ram and sacrificed it as a burnt offering instead of his son." Thus "Abraham called that place The LORD Will Provide," a saying that has been preserved to this day as a proverb and a promise: "On the mountain of the LORD it will be provided."

So, what of Abraham's stern "test"? What does it mean for me?

It comes to this: Can I endure the loss of anything I deem essential to life and believe that "in this place" of death and grief my God can and will provide?

I think of this as I stare in stark unbelief at what God is asking some of my friends to endure: critical illness, crippling infirmity, isolation and dislocation, the inability to use the talents and abilities with which they hoped to serve God to the end of their days. "Is this what He is asking of *me*?" my heart cries out.

Yet I know that there is love and logic in all God will ask of me. My losses—whatever they may be—are to the end that He may use me in a greater way to bring glory to His name and salvation to the world. Thus God swore to Abraham: "Because you have done this and have not withheld your son, your only son, I will surely bless you and make your descendants as numerous as the stars in the sky and as the sand on the seashore. Your descendants will take possession of the cities of their enemies, and through your offspring all nations on earth will be blessed, because you have obeyed me."

Now, God said to Abraham, the fruitfulness of your life will be manifest.

When you and I come to "the place" where we offer up all that we are and have to God—even the best gifts He has given us—*then* we will become a blessing to everyone we touch. This is the record of all whose lives have counted for God. Is this not what Jesus meant when He promised, "Whoever loses his life for my sake will find it" (Matthew 10:39)?

AN AFTERTHOUGHT...

I cannot leave this story without mentioning that David purchased Moriah from Aravnah the Canaanite to mark the place where Abraham offered up Isaac. It was there that Solomon built the temple. Moriah is not a single peak, but an elongated ridge that begins at the junction of the Kidron and Hinnom Valleys and rises to its summit just northwest of the present Damascus Gate. There is sound archeological evidence to suppose that Jesus was crucified there on the summit, "on that place." And I fail to see how anyone reading about old Abraham, leading his dear son up the flanks of Mount Moriah, binding him to the altar while his heart breaks within him, can fail to miss the parallel with God leading His own Son to that same mountain centuries later "to the place of the Skull" (John 19:17). There He made the provision upon which all other provisions are based.

Did Abraham know? Perhaps this is what Jesus meant when He said, "Abraham rejoiced at the thought of seeing my day; he saw it *and was glad*" (John 8:56).

BIRD SONG

Field and forest, vale and mountain,
Flow'ry meadow, flashing sea,
Chanting bird and flowing fountain
Call us to rejoice in Thee.

—GENEVAN PSALTER

Solomon describes old age as a time "when men rise up at the sound of birds, but all their songs grow faint" (Ecclesiastes 12:4). He was right, of course, on both counts: I get up with the birds, but until I get my bearings and my hearing aid in place, I can't hear their songs. Thanks to the marvel of modern gadgetry, however, I *can* hear birds quite well these days, and their singing makes my heart swell with joy.

I read the other day that birds sing "because they can and because they must. Songs are used to attract mates and defend territories, but the form is much more than function. Nature is full of beauty, and of music." So writes David Rothenberg, a professor at New Jersey Institute of Technology.

The professor goes on to explain that birds sing because they have a syrinx instead of a larynx. The syrinx is a unique musical instrument that looks like a hollow, inverted Y that lies deep in a bird's chest at the point where the trachea divides into the two bronchia which rise from the lungs. Each leg of the Y rests on a separate bronchial tube, thus giving birds unusual control and creativity in the sounds they can make.

Birds can sing two different notes at the same time, or sing a duet with themselves. They are capable of singing a rising note with one side of the syrinx and a falling note with the other. They can use one side for low notes and the other for high ones, or switch from one side to the other in mid-note. No other creature is quite so versatile.

But what I ask is, *why* do birds sing—really? Why these tiny virtuosos? Why does "the air tremble with the din of songs and the whir of wings"?

Birds were brought into being before us to fill the earth with joyful music—to draw our hearts up to God in thanksgiving and adoration. Birds are "heaven's high and holy muses," John Donne said, daily reminders that God has given *us* a song so we may sing with them in praise and thanksgiving to our creator.

We can sing along with Israel's sweet singer:

> *"I will sing of your strength,*
> *in the morning I will sing of your love;*
> *for you are my fortress,*
> *my refuge in times of trouble."*

PSALM 59:16

We can "sing of the ways of the LORD, for the glory of the LORD is great" (Psalm 138:5). We can "sing . . . for [the LORD] has done marvelous things; his right hand and his holy arm have worked salvation for [us]" (Psalm 98:1). Or we can make up our very own song!

So, when you hear God's little hymn-birds break into carefree song each morning, echo their melodies with your own. Lift up your voice—harmonious, hoarse, or harsh—and join them in praise to your Creator, Redeemer, and Lord. Sing from your soul-nest.

But, you say, "I don't feel like singing this morning." All is still—no flutter, no melody? Sing anyway. There is grace sufficient to sing, and joy may surprise you as you make melody in your heart to the Lord. Give it a try. What do you have to lose but your sorrow?

Israel's poet observed:

> *"The birds of the air nest by the waters;*
> *they sing among the branches . . .*
> *[Therefore] I will sing to the LORD all my life;*
> *I will sing praise to my God as long as I live."*

> PSALM 104:12, 33

COUNTING
THE DAYS

That flesh is but the [hour] glasse,
which holds the dust
That measures all our time.

—GEORGE HERBERT

Psalm 90 is "A Prayer of Moses," the wistful reflections and petitions of an old man. Here Moses, as Flannery O'Connor once pointed out, is in the most significant position life offers us: He is facing death.

Moses begins by pondering the vast difference between God and His creatures. He is eternal; we are not. He is "from everlasting to everlasting." We are ephemeral, swept away "in the sleep of death." We spring up like grass in the morning and by evening we are withered and dry, a little mound of dust.

"Why do we have to die?" I ask myself. God has put eternity in our hearts; we were made for immortality! Why does death sweep us away?

The answer comes as a complete surprise: Death is not our lot; it is our sentence. We are "consumed by [God's] anger." We are mortal because we are sinful. "The wages of sin is death" (Romans 6:23).

To use Moses' words, we are "hurried away" by God's indignation, which is why, I suppose, we keep looking at our watches (see Psalm 90:7—the Hebrew verb here has this connotation). The "span" of our days passes quickly: *tempus fugit* (time flies), we say. No, "*we* fly away" (Psalm 90:10). As the old Isaac Watts hymn puts it:

> *Time, like an ever-rolling stream,*
> *Bears all its sons away;*
> *They fly forgotten as a dream*
> *Dies at the op'ning day.*

So, I say to myself, it's a good thing to ponder the brevity of life now and then, and to number my days, as Moses suggests. Three-score and ten years are allotted, or four-score if I'm unduly strong. But in the end the grave gets us all.

I have to say, we don't think much about dying these days. In earlier times folks were more comfortable with the idea. Churches were surrounded by cemeteries and filled with sepulchers—somber reminders that one's body would one day lie under a slab. The village parson, George Herbert, said he frequented graveyards to "take acquaintance of this heap of dust." Today, we want cemeteries to be out of town or out of sight, out of mind, as far away as possible.

So, what will take away our fear of death? It is a promise of a "morning" that rends the skies, when we rise from "the sleep of death" that has swept us away (compare Psalm 90:14 with 90:5). This is the promise of the resurrection—a prospect that is a spring of invincible joy, a current of mirth under all our troubles. We can, as Moses insists, "be glad *all* our days" (Psalm 90:14).

So for the rest of our days on earth, we pray with Moses: "May the favor of the Lord our God rest upon us; establish [make permanent] the work of our hands for us" (Psalm 90:17). And may God direct us to do those things that have eternal significance: prayer, love, purity, wisdom, and quiet proclamation.

We pass through this world and on, like a swallow through a loft, but our influence can be eternal. We may not live long, but we can "live deep," as a friend of mine says. Then, when I have served God's purposes in my generation, I can fly away (see Acts 13:36).

There was a needlepoint plaque that hung on a wall in the home in which I grew up. (Thank you, Mother.) It meant very little to me then; it means a good deal to me now:

> *Only one life, 'twill soon be past;*
> *Only what's done for Christ will last.*
> *And when I am dying, how glad I will be,*
> *That the lamp of my life has blazed out for Thee.*

DANGEROUS
CROSSINGS

*Life is mighty chancy at
any kind of trade.*

—RUDYARD KIPLING

I don't wade swift streams any more, even when the best fishing lies on the other side of the river. The rocks are too slippery, the currents are too strong, my balance is too uncertain, and my old legs aren't what they used to be.

I take this as a parable for my life: So many challenges I once took on readily are now too challenging for me. Like the psalmist, I lose sleep at night wondering how I can negotiate them (see Psalm 77:1–4).

But then I remember the deeds of the Lord. He led His "people like a flock." Like a good shepherd He brought all Israel safely through the Red Sea to the other side. His "path led through the sea, [His] way through the mighty waters" (see Psalm 77:19–20 here and for the rest of the Scripture references in this chapter). No one was left behind, no one was abandoned, no one was swept away. God surged through the Red Sea as I would wade a tiny brook.

All of us face difficult and dangerous crossings in our lifetime—a transition to a new place or position, a decision to abandon a sinful practice and make a new beginning, a choice to walk a way we would rather not go, a call to venture ourselves in untried service, a retirement that takes us from prominence to a lower profile, or our final crossing through the river "bitter and cold." Yet we need not fear the dark currents, for God does not fear them. His strength and courage are infinite. He will see us through.

The psalmist observes, with some wonderment, that God leaves no footprints as He accompanies us. Just as the sand in the bottom of a stream hides our footprints as soon as they are imprinted, so God's presence, as real as our own, is hidden from us. He is with us, "walking incognito," as C. S. Lewis said, and thus we may not realize He is present. But, Lewis continues, "the incognito is not hard to penetrate. The real labor is to remember, to attend. In fact, to come awake. Still more, to remain awake," to make ourselves think about His presence, to remind ourselves that He is at our side.

Furthermore, though we cannot see God's footprints in our crossings, He is incarnate in human agents that we can see. At the Red Sea He led Israel "by the hand of Moses and Aaron." Think back to how He has led you—in the wise counsel of a mother, in the strong grip of a father, in the urgings of godly brother or sister, in the quiet encouragement of a caring spouse, in the gentle touch of a child.

How many hands have reached out to us—guiding us, encouraging us, strengthening us? In them we perceive the hand of our Lord leading us through deep and dangerous waters to the other side.

Hard crossings are inevitable, but our Lord has promised: "When you pass through the waters, I will be with you; and when you pass through the rivers, they will not sweep over you" (Isaiah 43:2).

> I came to the swift, raging river,
> And the roar held the echo of fear;
> "Oh, Lord, give me wings to fly over,
> If You are, as You promised, quite near."

But He said, "Trust the grace I am giving,
All-pervasive, sufficient for you.
Take My hand—we will face it together,
But My plan is not over but through."

—LEE WEBBER

IS THIS ALL THE THANKS I GET?

Teach me, Lord, not to gather encouragement from
appreciation by others, lest this should interfere with purity of
motive—not to seek praise, respect, gratitude, or regard from
superiors or equals on account of age, or past service.

—EDWARD BENSON from *Prayers, Public and Private*

For several years my wife Carolyn and I, somewhat like Job, sat in a "Nash heap"—a 1959, porcelain-white Nash Rambler station wagon that looked for all the world like an inverted bathtub on wheels. If it were turned upside down, I could have clamped an outboard motor on the rear bumper and raced the thing in Vancouver's annual Nanaimo Bathtub Regatta.

I still remember the day we began visiting car lots to replace it. We looked at a number of shiny new vehicles and finally decided on a purchase. Unfortunately, the payments were more than we could carry.

We dickered for a while with the salesman—his price and ours—but concluded that the twain would never meet and hastened to make our departure. As we were leaving his office, the salesman gave us his best shot. "Hey, you guys deserve this car," he shouted. In my heart of hearts I responded, "Indeed we do!"

Entitlement has always been one of my soft spots. "I've been a pretty good guy," I say to myself. "My accomplishments deserve a bit of praise." Which is why I get my nose out of joint when people don't appreciate me.

Then one day I came upon God's word to Zechariah about a shepherd who dedicated himself to the good of his people, who encouraged peace, prosperity, and brought tranquility and harmony to his flock. He, however, far from being appreciated, was despised and rejected. Those who discarded him set his price at thirty pieces of silver, the value of a slave (Zechariah 11:7–13). Should I expect more?

And then there is Solomon's tale of "a small city with only a few people in it, and a powerful king who . . . surrounded it and built huge siege works against it." But, "there lived in that city a man poor but wise, and he saved the city by his wisdom." Let's hear it for the wise man! What will he receive for his efforts? Alas, "nobody remembered that poor man" (Ecclesiastes 9:14–15).

One of the things I'm learning as I grow older is not to expect too much from people. It's possible to pour a good deal of effort, energy, and love into a friend or family member and receive nothing but ingratitude for our efforts. It's even possible that others may receive credit for the good that we've done.

We should all express appreciation to those who come to our side, but if we expect everyone to recognize what we have done for them, we can be deeply hurt. And we'll soon be asking ourselves: "Is this all the thanks I get?"

It's good, in those times of disappointment, to look into our own motives: Do we have an unholy sense of entitlement, or a passion to be seen and applauded for our efforts? Can we give freely and allow others to take responsibility for their own responses?

There are grateful men and women in this world, and we may hear from them. But the statistics in Jesus' parable of the ten virgins suggest that perhaps only ten percent of those we love and serve will ever thank us. The others will be silent at best. At worst they may be hostile. So if even one has responded, be grateful. And remember—God *alone* enables us to do good things for others.

> *And if the love of a grateful heart*
> *As a rich reward be given,*
> *Lift thou the love of a grateful heart*
> *To the God of Love in Heaven.*
>
> —GEORGE MACDONALD, *"Lessons for a Child"*

Ingratitude in others can embitter us if we're not watchful. We must forgive those who fail to thank us—even those who, despite the love we've bestowed upon them, have turned away from us. Jesus said, "Love your enemies, do good to them, and lend to them *without expecting to get anything back.* Then your reward will be great, and you will be sons of the Most High, because he is kind to the *ungrateful . . .*" (Luke 6:35, emphasis added).

Our Lord will be "kind" to *us* when we see Him face to face, for we too have been ungrateful. His "well-done" will ring throughout the universe, and He will praise us before human beings and angels. This may be the only appreciation we receive for the good we've done on earth, but in the end it's the only praise that will matter.

And though we cannot do much about those who disregard us, we can do a good deal about ourselves. Sometimes in the busyness of our lives we fail to express the appreciation to those who have contributed so much to us—parents, spouses, siblings, friends, teachers, mentors, colleagues, to name only a few. Yet it doesn't take much time or effort to express our gratitude—a brief but heartfelt word of appreciation, a phone call, a text message, an e–mail, or a thank-you note will do.

Speaking of which, Carolyn and I have often marveled at our culture's indifference to thank-you notes. "I don't write little thank-you notes," a man said recently in our hearing. We could only stare in amazement. Is this refinement and courtesy so frivolous that it's now beneath us?

"Sending thank-you notes has become a lost art," mourns Mary Mitchell, a syndicated columnist who writes under the name of Ms. *Demeanor*. "A grateful attitude is a tremendous life skill, and an efficient and inexpensive way to set ourselves apart in the work force and in our adult lives . . . The habit of manners comes from inside—it's an attitude based on respecting other people."

Appreciation is an attitude based on respect for other people, even the unkind and ungrateful. But primarily it is an attitude based on love, for "love has good manners" (1 Corinthians 13:5 NKJV: "Does not behave rudely."). And the habit of thankfulness must come from inside, for gratitude is the work of God's Holy Spirit. Apart from His grace, we would all be ungrateful wretches.

GOING AND NOT KNOWING

God of the coming years,
through paths unknown we follow Thee.

—HUGH T. KERR

Abraham was seventy-five years of age when he was taken from his home in Ur of the Chaldees. His entire life from that time on became nomadic as he moved from one place to another —from Ur to Haran, to Shechem, to Bethel, to Egypt, to the Negev, to Hebron . . . "By faith Abraham . . . obeyed and went, even though he did not know where he was going" (Hebrews 11:8). Rootless, homeless, going and not knowing—that was the story of his life.

In thinking about Abraham's changing environment, it occurred to me that aging itself is a journey away from settled and secure places to endless change, uncertainty, and adjustment. It is transition from a familiar past to an uncertain future. It is movement from a family home, to a smaller place, to a daughter's home, to a retirement community, to a nursing home—the "last resort," as a friend of mine says. Sociologist Paul Tournier describes the experience as always being "in between," like a trapeze artist suspended in mid-air.

So, like Abraham, as we grow older we pass "through paths unknown," making our way from one place to another, always traveling, going and not knowing, "just lookin' for a home." Yet we can be at home in every place we dwell, for our safekeeping lies not in the place, but in God himself. He is our home and our habitation. We dwell in the shelter of the Most High. We rest in the shadow of the Almighty (Psalm 91:1, 9).

It is noteworthy that Abraham raised a rough-hewn altar in every place he lived. There, we're told, he "called on the name of the Lord"— he bowed his heart in worship.

Worship is the way we get our minds off our circumstances and ourselves and give our full attention to God. There, in His presence, under His wings, we find refuge. The eternal God becomes our dwelling place (Psalm 90:1).

Peter was told, "When you are old you will stretch out your hands, and someone else will dress you and lead you where you do not want to go." Nevertheless, Jesus called to him, "Follow me!" (John 21:18–19).

Though it may seem that others are choosing our habitation, it is our sovereign Lord who actually makes these choices, leading us from one place to another. He will turn each dreary dwelling place into a house of grace in which we can shed the light of God's lovingkindness on other travelers. And He will be our companion and friend until our traveling days are over and we reach our heart's true Home.

God of the coming years, through paths unknown
we follow Thee.

WEARINESS

More life I need ere I myself can be.
Sometimes, when the eternal tide ebbs low,
A moment weary of my life I grow.

—GEORGE MACDONALD, *Diary of an Old Soul*

What is this weariness that settles upon us as we age? Does it come from something that needs to be set right?

Not necessarily. Sin does wear us out. The burden of guilt and shame is a heavy load to bear. But it may not be evil-doing that weighs us down. We may be "weary in well-doing," as Paul would say, for love can be hard work that wears out both body and soul. Or, our weariness may be the sin of another and our inability to give help as we would like to do. Or it may come simply from prolonged illness or pain.

I delight in George MacDonald's *Diary of an Old Soul,* for my old soul resonates so readily with his. There he writes:

Shall fruit be blamed if it hang wearily
A day before it perfected drop plumb
To the sad earth from off its nursing tree?
Ripeness must always come with loss of might.
The weary evening fall before the resting night.

Weariness and "loss of might" bring ripeness, for they remind us that we're passing away so that a better thing may come. The weary evening leads to the resting night. This is what we Christians call "hope," and in this hope we renew our souls, as the prophet Isaiah declares.

> [Our] Lord is the everlasting God,
> the Creator of the ends of the earth.
> He will not grow tired or weary,
> and his understanding no one can fathom.
> He gives strength to the weary
> and increases the power of the weak.
> Even youths grow tired and weary,
> and young men stumble and fall;
> but those who hope in the Lord
> will renew their strength.
> They will soar on wings like eagles;
> they will run and not grow weary,
> they will walk and not be faint.
>
> ISAIAH 40:28–31

Hope, Isaiah's strong word, looks to the future. It is waiting in confidence for a salvation that is certain to come—kept in heaven for those who are themselves kept for the day of salvation.

This is the perspective that overwhelms my weariness; not accidentally, but essentially, for if I know that my ultimate destiny is glorious, it picks up my pace here and now. I can stretch the wings of my heart and fly! I can run in the path of obedience and not get tired. I can walk through routine, pedestrian days and not grow weary.

The spirit is willing, but the flesh is weak, I say; but a better world is coming in which my spirit will call me to action and my body will run and leap and fly! This is my assurance, for hope, in biblical terms, does not imply contingency but certainty. As a backcountry friend of mine once put it, "My salvation is for certain sure!"

In the meantime, what someday will be true can begin to be true even now. I can be steadfast, patient, and joyful in spite of my deep weariness; kind and calm, less focused on my own frailty and fatigue; more concerned about others than I am about myself—and thus able "to speak a word in season to him that is weary" (Isaiah 50:4 KJV).

A RIVER RUNS THROUGH US

Their leaves will not wither,
nor will their fruit fail.
Every month they will bear,
because the water from the sanctuary
flows to them. Their fruit will serve for food
and their leaves for healing.

—EZEKIEL 47:12

I love to stroll alongside Idaho's brooks and streams that run like veins of silver through this beautiful land. But in all my days—and I've been around awhile—I've never seen a river like the one Ezekiel saw (Ezekiel 47:1–13).

The prophet, in a vision, was touring the temple in Jerusalem, accompanied by an angelic companion, when he came upon a rivulet flowing from under the threshold of the temple—just a trickle. Ezekiel traced the tiny stream to its source and discovered a spring bubbling up from the ground from under the brazen altar, the place of sacrifice.

Ezekiel's companion then led him outside the walls of the city and downstream to the place where the river flowed off the flanks of Mount Zion toward the east. The angel had a measuring stick in his hand, and as he walked he measured off the distance.

Ezekiel and his friend walked a little less than a quarter of a mile, and the angel led Ezekiel into the water. It was ankle-deep.

The angel then paced off the same distance and led Ezekiel into the water. It was knee-deep.

He measured off the distance again and led Ezekiel into the river. The water was up to his waist.

The angel measured off the distance and led Ezekiel into the river again. The water was over his head, a river "deep enough to swim in—a river that no-one could cross."

Then Ezekiel saw the region to which the river flowed: a dead sea that was made alive! Great schools of fish were swimming in its waters; fishermen were crowding its banks; trees were growing in profusion along its shores—"because the water from the sanctuary flows to them."

First a sanctuary, then an altar, and then a stream trickling out from under the altar that gets wider and deeper as it flows—an inexhaustible, copious supply that takes away bitterness and makes the land sweet and fruitful. All because a river flows through it.

There are no rivers on earth like Ezekiel's stream—no streams that begin as a trickle and get wider and deeper without tributaries or underground springs. We ask ourselves, as Ezekiel's companion asked, "Do you *see* this?"

If we take the trouble to trace the little stream to its source, we find an altar, a place of sacrifice on which the Lamb of God was slain. Underneath the altar there is a spring that bubbles up from the ground, a hidden source, a fountain of life.

Jesus said, "If anyone is thirsty, let him come to me and drink. Whoever believes in me, as the Scripture has said, streams of living water will flow from within him" (John 7:37–38). He alone is the living water for which we thirst, a fountain in the heart that becomes a river that flows deep and wide, a river that rises and floods, that empties into *our* dead seas, that dispels our dearth, filling our days with singing and laughter. "Where the river flows there is life!"

Are you weary in your love? Do you need new tenderness, compassion, and concern for those around you? Stoop down and drink from the hidden springs of God's love. Deepen your union with Him by prayer and devotion. He will be a spring of living water, of enduring, self-effacing love, rising up in you.

Are there demands on your time and energy that drain you until you have nothing left to give? Keep opening your heart to God. Pray over His Word and meditate on it day and night. New thoughts will spring up, fruit for food and leaves for healing. All your fresh springs are in Him (see Ezekiel 47:12 and Psalm 87:7).

Are you weary of the struggle in your spiritual life? Do you seek a quiet, more restful progress, or a refreshment for the wilderness and waste places of your life? This too comes from God, for the life we live is not ours, but His. He is in us, a never-ending source of righteousness, joy, and peace. "Where [God's] river flows there is life!" There is no other source.

"Whoever is thirsty, let him come; and whoever wishes, let him take the free gift of the water of life" (Revelation 22:17). There is no cost, for Love paid the price on Calvary. There is only one requirement: We must *thirst*. Everyone who thirsts,

> *Come to the waters;*
> *And you who have no money,*
> *Come, buy and eat.*
> *Yes, come, buy wine and milk*
> *Without money and without price.*

Why do you spend money for what is not bread,
And your wages for what does not satisfy?
Listen carefully to Me, and eat what is good,
And let your soul delight itself in abundance.

ISAIAH 55:1–2 NKJV

THE HILL
DIFFICULTY

He who has compassion on them
will guide them and lead them
beside springs of water.

—ISAIAH 49:10

There is a glacial lake that lies high in a fold of Jug Handle Peak in the mountains north of our home in Boise. It's a dot on the map, but a place of rare beauty and tranquility for me.

The route to the lake takes me up a steep, exposed ridge through boulders and scree. It's a strenuous ascent—hard on my old heart and legs. In the summer, the sun beats down mercilessly on my head, and there's no shade to be found anywhere. At the bottom of the climb, however, there's a brook—a spring that seeps out of soft, mossy earth and flows through a lush meadow crammed with flowers that bloom in wild profusion. It's a quiet place to hydrate myself and prepare for the hard climb that lies ahead.

This reminds me of the moment in *The Pilgrim's Progress* when Christian and his fellow-travelers find themselves at the foot of another steep ascent, the Hill Difficulty, at the bottom of which there is a spring. "Christian now went to the spring and drank thereof to refresh himself, and then began to go up the hill."

Perhaps you, too, stand at the foot of Hill Difficulty facing an impossibly high mountain to be climbed, a challenge that cannot be met through mere strength or wisdom. Perhaps your mountain is the care of an aging or disabled spouse, a difficult financial decision—one on which your earthly future depends—or a painful recovery from a surgical procedure. The demands seem insurmountable.

Before you do anything else, visit the spring that is God himself. Come to Him with all your weakness, weariness, helplessness, failure, doubt, and fear. Drink deeply of His power and wisdom; fill yourself full of His everlasting love. (Dehydration imperils the body *and* soul.) Ask for faith and hardy endurance to face and surmount the difficulty. (To ask is to receive.)

Whatever we have to do, God must perfect it. He knows all our circumstances and supplies us *ahead of time* with a store of comfort, of spiritual strengthening and consolation, that we may have ready at hand, that we can resort to and lay up in our heart as an antidote against despair.[1]

We drink from the spring from which our Lord himself drank when He stood at the foot of Hill Calvary—"a brook beside the way" (Psalm 110:7). Then, rested and refreshed, having set the Lord before us, we can rise and face the difficulty that looms ahead.

The mountain may remain, as demanding as ever. But forearmed with prevenient grace—God's goodness and mercy that precedes all human effort—we can ascend with steady faith, hope, and love.

---

[1] Sir Thomas More, A *Dialogue of Comfort Against Tribulation,* written just before he ascended Hill Difficulty—his martyrdom in 1535. The exact quotation from the original is: "I will supply you ahead of time with a store of comfort, of spiritual strengthening and consolation, that you can have ready at hand, that you can resort to and lay up in your heart as an antidote against the poison of despairing dread."

A RUIN! A RUIN! A RUIN!

He took the silver and the gold,
To make me rich in grace;
He quenched earth's lights that I might see
The shining of his face.

—F. B. MEYER

I was hiking in the mountains south of our home in Boise several months ago and came across the ruins of the Golden Chariot Mine, one of the richest gold mines in the Owyhee Mountains of Idaho. I had read that it was the cause of a bitter war that raged underground for weeks—a bloody gun battle in which a number of men lost their lives. The gold still lies in a rich vein that runs under War Eagle Mountain, yet the mine, and all that men gave their lives for there, remains in ruins.

"A ruin! A ruin! I will make it a ruin," Ezekiel exclaims, using the strongest superlative in the Hebrew language. "It will not be restored until he comes to whom it rightfully belongs" (see Ezekiel 21:18–27).

This prophecy was directed against Zedekiah, the king of Judah, and was a prediction of the siege of Jerusalem and its destruction by Nebuchadnezzar and his army.

Jerusalem was impregnable, or so Zedekiah believed, his place of ultimate safety. Its walls would never fall. Yet, as the prophecy foretold, the city in which he placed his trust would be reduced to ruins and would not be fully restored, "until He comes to whom it rightfully belongs."

This reference goes back a thousand years or more to Jacob's ancient prophecy: "The scepter will not depart from Judah, nor the ruler's staff from between his feet, *until he comes to whom it belongs* and the obedience of the nations is his" (Genesis 49:10, emphasis added). This is the promise of Israel's Messiah, the one to whom the kingdom rightfully belonged. It was this reminder and the destruction of the city of Jerusalem that awakened God's people once again to their need for His wise and righteous rule and His promise that He would restore the city's glory and beauty.

Ruin comes to all of us so that God may build a better thing. He shakes what can be shaken, so that what cannot be shaken may remain. This is the hidden meaning of the devastation that brings down the things we've given our lives to build up and to maintain.

When we fall into ruin, God has graciously provided a way to rebuild. We may live with the results of our sin, but sin repented of draws us back into God's great heart and enables Him to restore us. The grace of men is a sometime thing; the grace of God endures forever.

God's grace is determined by His interest in us. He uses everything for *our* greater good, even our ruin. This is what theologians call "the economy of salvation." God wastes nothing, not even our sin. "God knows how to draw glory even from our faults. Not to be downcast after committing a fault is one of the marks of true sanctity" (Augustine Guillard).

We must not let our defeats defeat us, for our defilement and God's forgiving grace can become the means by which we are drawn into an intimacy with our Lord in greater measure than before. Our sin—repented of and put away—can result in greater results for the kingdom of

God than anything we could have accomplished otherwise. Grace takes our most depraved and black-hearted sin and turns it into something beautiful for Him. That, and not our sin, is the final word.

God rids our hearts of past sorrow, even as His goodness and love treat our sins as if they had never happened. And then, as David assures us, "He leads us in paths of righteousness."

The retirement funds we've accumulated with so much care are lost that we may acquire better riches. The reputation we've established for integrity and restraint is shattered that we may despair of our own goodness and find our righteousness in Christ. The friendships we've cultivated lie in ruins that we may gain a truer Friend. The love of our life is taken away that a greater Love may possess us. And then there is aging, the thing that eventually ruins all of us. We are brought down, rendered useless, stripped of pretense and defenses so God can build from the ground up. As George MacDonald said, we learn "to live without earthly provision or precaution." God becomes our sole good, the only thing we desire.

In the end our ruination will have become the best thing that ever happened to us, for it will have turned us to the One to whom we rightfully belong—and in so doing we are restored.

THE DISCIPLINE OF DISTRESS

If "the nightingale sings best
with a thorn against her breast,"
why not we?

—SUSAN GILBERT DICKINSON
in a letter to Emily Dickinson (1861)

Suffering is exact. We don't grieve in general or in the abstract, but in specific, concrete ways. Most of the consolation we receive, however, is loaded with generalizations and abstractions, as anyone who has ever received a sympathy card knows. "It's all for the best," our friends assure us. Or, "It will turn out for good."

Such comfort, however well-meant, is ineffective. When I suffer, I crave an answer as precise as my pain. In what sense is my suffering for the best? And what is the good, if any, to which my suffering will be turned?

God is fair and just, although the final explanation for evil and injustice awaits heaven. I cannot know every purpose for which God permits trouble to come my way, and I would be foolish to give an unequivocal answer to the question, "Why suffering?" Yet my afflictions are not meaningless. They are part of the specific good God has determined to do: namely, to turn me to His Word for His discipline and instruction that He may enlighten and deepen me.

The psalmist's argument in Psalm 94 is clear: "How long will the wicked [go unpunished]?" he asks. And God answers: "Does he who *disciplines* nations not punish? Does he who *teaches* man lack knowledge [of their evil]?" (Psalm 94:3, 10, emphasis added). God will discipline the ungodly in due time, He insists; but first He must *discipline* and *teach* His own children. A good father begins with his own family (1 Peter 4:17).

Affliction, when we accept it with humility, can be instructive, a discipline that leads us to a deeper, fuller life. "Before I was afflicted I went astray," the psalmist says, "but now I obey your word." And again, "It was good for me to be afflicted so that I might learn your decrees." Peter would agree. Affliction, he says, leads us to live no longer for ourselves, but "for the will of God" (Psalm 110:67, 71; 1 Peter 4:2).

Pain, far from being an obstacle to our spiritual growth, can be the condition of it—if we're trained by it. It pushes us closer to God and into His Word. It is the means by which He graciously shapes us to be like His Son, gradually giving us the compassion, contentment, tranquility, and courage we long and pray for. Without pain, God could never make the most of our lives.

That's why Job, who suffered more than anyone I can name, exclaimed in the midst of his troubles, "Blessed is the man whom God corrects," though admittedly, he, like us, found it hard to sustain that thesis at all times (Job 5:17).

Are you one whom God has set apart today to instruct through suffering and pain? Endure His discipline patiently. He can make the trial a blessing, using it to draw you into His heart and into His Word, teaching you the lessons He intends you to learn, working in you the grace He means to bestow, giving you "respite from days of trouble" (Psalm 94:13). This is the "good" to which your suffering can be turned (Romans 8:28–29).

God is making more out of you than you ever thought possible.

> *Consider it pure joy, my brothers, whenever you face trials of many kinds, because you know that the testing of your faith develops perseverance.*

JAMES 1:2–3

PRESSING ON

If I do not experience something
far worse than I yet have done,
I shall say the trouble is all in getting started.

—MRS. GEORGE (TAMSEN E.) DONNER,
member of the ill-fated Donner party,
in a letter dated June 16, 1846

Every age has its perils, but the greatest peril may be in thinking that the trouble "is all in getting started." Sometimes the greatest hazards lie ahead.

Noah, Moses, Gideon, Samuel, David, Solomon, Uzziah, and a host of biblical people fell into failure near the end of their days. As the apostle Paul reminds us, "If you think you are standing firm, be careful that you don't fall!" (1 Corinthians 10:12).

"The long, dull, monotonous years of middle-aged prosperity or middle-aged adversity are excellent campaigning weather for the devil," C. S. Lewis wrote in *The Screwtape Letters*. And the devil's finest stratagem is sloth, "that great, sprawling, slug-a-bed sin," as Dorothy Sayers termed it.

Sloth is a spiritual indifference or apathy that has many causes, but may grow out of the belief that we've arrived and have no more ground to gain. Or, that we have little left to give. "Apathy causes one to fall into a deep sleep," the Wise Man said, and then added, "that soul will go hungry" (Proverbs 19:15, my translation). Ah, there it is: a spiritual torpor that starves our souls. Slow down, we say to ourselves; you've given much. Isn't it time to refrain from further sacrifice? Spare yourself. Why go on reading, studying, pursuing God. Stop this strenuous following after.

No! I say. That is not true. We can never stop growing toward God. Holiness is a dynamic thing, a matter of motion. There is no static balance in the spiritual life. We're either moving toward God or away from Him.

St. Gregory put it simply: "When the soul does not direct its efforts to higher things . . . it stoops to concern itself with low desires." When we fail to direct our passions toward heavenly things, we fall into ungodly desires. Bitter animosities demean us; irritability, petulance, impatience, and loss of temper degrade our souls.

So we must never let up, for our adversary does not. He is working every moment to plague and blight our final years. We must pursue God and His righteousness with hearty energy to the end of our days. This was Paul's driving compulsion: "To know Christ and the power of his resurrection and the fellowship of sharing in his sufferings, becoming like him in his death" (Philippians 3:10). It must be ours as well.

To know Jesus, to experience more of his life-giving power, to patiently bear our portion of His humiliation and suffering, to become like Him in self-sacrificing love—this is the work that must keep us busy to the end of our days.

We'll not "achieve" the righteousness we seek in this life—that awaits heaven—but you and I must "*press on* to take hold of that for which Christ Jesus took hold of [us]" (Philippians 3:12, emphasis added).

So, we must pursue the Lord and His righteousness with all our heart, soul, and mind—with a fierce, unyielding resolve for as many days as He may give us. We must spend time in His presence and choose to do His will. Thus He will fill us with His Spirit and deliver us from the perils that lie ahead.

THE YOKE

Who best bear his mild yoke,
they serve him best.

—JOHN MILTON, "On His Blindness"

There was an occasion on which Judah's king, Zedekiah, and a number of dignitaries from surrounding nations gathered in Jerusalem to plot rebellion against Babylon (see Jeremiah 27:1–15).

Jeremiah the prophet, who was always unpredictable, crashed the party, bearing a heavy wooden yoke on his shoulders and offering this explanation: "'Bow your neck under the yoke of the king of Babylon; serve him and his people, and you will live'" (Jeremiah 27:12).

History proved him right. Those who patiently endured Babylon's yoke lived in Jerusalem in peace and safety; those who resisted lost their lives. (You can read the record in 2 Kings 24:1–25:30.)

Jeremiah elsewhere said of his own transgressions: "'My sins have been bound into a yoke; by his hands they were woven together. They have come upon my neck and the Lord has sapped my strength. He has handed me over to those I cannot withstand'" (Lamentations 1:14).

I think of those who have sinned recklessly in their youth and who now must bear the consequences—an alienated family, a ruined reputation, a sexually transmitted disease. Although the sin itself, if confessed and repented of, has been fully forgiven, the sad consequences of sins may linger on and on.

Have your sins been bound into a yoke that causes great grief? If so, "bow your neck under the yoke" and bear it patiently. Let God determine the time and the terms of the burden you bear and rely on His mercy, remembering that all things, even the dire consequences of your sins, flow out of His wisdom and love.

The yoke may cause great grief, but resistance only leads to greater discomfort. We must endure the hardship of discipline (Hebrews 12:7). We must learn the lessons of faith and patience that are found in the burden. This, and not escape, leads to "an eternal glory that far outweighs them all" (2 Corinthians 4:17).

God is not punitive. He disciplines us "for our good, that we may share in his holiness" (Hebrews 12:10). Pain and sorrow become the means by which He frees us from our preoccupation with earthly things and turns our hearts to unseen, eternal realities. He searches into our character and reveals its flaws so that His likeness may grow within us. And thus we come to the end of ourselves that we may share His glory.

Though chastened, we'll not be overwhelmed; though corrected and diminished, God will not "finish [us] off," for He has "more work left to do" on us (Jeremiah 46:28, *The Message*). And in His time, when His holy work is done, He will lift the burden from our shoulders—in this world or in the next.

In the meantime, we must pray for those we've damaged by our sin, knowing that God can bring good even from the suffering we've inflicted on others.

Finally, we must not grow anxious about those whom God is using to chafe us. They may go beyond His boundaries, as Nebuchadnezzar did, but their time will come (Jeremiah 27:7). There's no need to quarrel or contend with them, or to take their judgment into our hands. We must leave them to God, the judge of all, and be at peace.

He will judge the world in righteousness
and the peoples in his truth.

PSALM 96:13

THE WORLD'S LAST NIGHT

The doctrine of the Second Coming has failed,
so far as we are concerned, if it does not make us realize
that at every moment of every year in our lives
Donne's question "What if this present were the
world's last night?" is equally relevant.

—C. S. LEWIS

I love to read old newspapers from the days of the Idaho frontier. One such paper is *The Owyhee Avalanche*, a chronicle that covered events in and around Owyhee County (the county to the south of us) in the mid to late nineteenth century.

On May 4, 1867, the paper carried this report: "James Fraser was shot and killed by Indians last Friday evening between sunset and dark." Fraser was a prospector working a gulch below Wagontown in the Owyhee Mountains of Idaho, closing in on pay dirt. He didn't plan to die that day... but he did. You just never know.

As Jeremy Taylor, a Church of England clergyman, wrote in the 1600s:

> Death meets us every where... and enters in at many
> doors. It enters by the fall of a chariot and the stumbling
> at a stone, by a full meal or an empty stomach, by
> watching at the wine or by watching at prayers, by the

sun or the moon, by a heat or a cold, by sleepless nights or sleeping days, by water frozen into the hardness and sharpness of a dagger, or water thawed into the floods of a river, by a hair or a raisin, by violent motion or sitting still, by severity or dissolution, by every thing in nature and every thing in chance.

The apostle Peter agrees. "The end of all things is near." (See 1 Peter 4:7–11 here and in the following references.) This night—tonight—may be "the world's last night"—at least for me. I may go to God this day, or He may come for me. This could be the last hour of my life.

So, I ask myself: How should I invest my time? What activities and attitudes should fill my final hours? Is there some magnificent gesture, some grand and glorious act to mark the end of my days?

First, I must *pray*: "Be clear minded and self-controlled so that you can pray," Peter writes. Prayer is my access to God, the way I can stay in touch with Him. It's not so much that prayer moves God, but that it moves me. It aligns me more closely with what He is doing, and conforms me to His will.

I must bring sobriety to prayer, Peter says. It's not that prayer must be joyless, for it can be whimsical, light-hearted, musical, full of mirth. No, what Peter inveighs against is superficiality. I must take *seriously* my need to fill my days with prayer because that is the secret of a useful, God-filled life—the means by which God can use me for the highest good. Without prayer I will accomplish exactly nothing.

And then I must *love* deeply—with great care and determination, "because love covers over a multitude of sins." Love and forgiveness mark me as God's child and remind others of His love. "No one can see God," John said, but they can see me.

Perhaps I can do nothing for a difficult neighbor, a struggling brother, a suffering friend. But I can love them. A smile, a note, a kind word, a brief touch can be the greatest thing in the world when I offer it in love. And even when my journey leads into illness, weakness, and infirmed old age, my work can be in loving, which in the end will be my greatest gift to God and to others.

In addition, I must *offer hospitality* to others without complaining. I can open my home and my heart to those in need; I can be available to *anyone* who happens to come my way. "Who is my neighbor?" Jesus answers: the next needy person you meet. I must keep my heart open to others and welcome all comers.

Then, I must use whatever gifts God has given me to *serve* others, "faithfully administering God's grace in its various forms." The gifts I have been given and the work I am called to do are from one mind. The God who made me made my path. For whatever days God gives me, I must put into practice His special design and purpose for me so I may live in loving service to Him and to others.

And finally, I must do all these things "with the strength God provides." God must put into me all that He wants to take out of me. I am nothing; He is everything. To *Him* be the glory (not me).

Prayer, love, hospitality, and humble service. How simple and how satisfying to do these things as though they are the last things I will do on earth. To do them lovingly, faithfully, patiently this day and the next day and the next day . . . If so, the last day will take care of itself.

It's never too late to get started; we're never too old to begin. "I must begin *today*!" (a phrase John Wesley is said to have often quoted to himself).

ON YAKS

We have been talking about faith ever since the Lord came.
It is not exhausted yet, and God forbid that I should think
that I know yet what faith is; although I know a little what it is.

—GEORGE MACDONALD,
"Faith, the Proof of the Unseen"

There's a yak," Carolyn said nonchalantly as we sped down the highway last summer. "Yeah, sure," I replied, with more irony in my voice than I intended.

"It *was* a yak!" Carolyn harrumphed. "I SAW IT WITH MY OWN EYES!" Then she lapsed into ominous silence.

"Well, there's one way to settle this matter," I muttered, and turned the car around and drove back to the place where she claimed to have seen the beast.

"There," she pointed, and exclaimed as the animal came into sight, "*See?* Now do you believe me?"

It was indeed a yak. I was chastened in my unbelief.

This exchange set me to thinking about faith and its properties. Like George MacDonald, I do not think that I know yet what faith is, but I learned a little what it is through that exchange. It occurs to me now that faith means believing *something*. But it is more. Faith is believing *someone*. Let me explain.

Faith, by biblical definition, is "being sure of what we hope for and certain of what we do not see" (Hebrews 11:1). Faith is unrestricted, unreserved, unconditional certainty. As Thomas Aquinas wrote, "It is part of the concept of belief itself that a man is *certain* of that in which he believes."

But that conviction is based on "things not seen" (Hebrews 11:1 NKJV). Faith's certainty does not rest on empirical, first-hand evidence, but on someone else's observations. When we have seen something for ourselves, we no longer believe; we "know." A "believer," then, in the strictest sense of the word, accepts a matter as real and true on the testimony of someone else.

I know, for example, that there was a yak on the road that day because I saw it with my own eyes. But if Carolyn tells me these days that she has seen another yak, while I may not *know* it, I will *believe* it (the fact of a yak); or, more exactly, I will believe *her*, for she has proved herself to be a credible witness.

Which brings me to the point of this chapter: I believe the stories about Jesus because I believe His apostles, who were eyewitnesses of the things He did and said; I believe that their firsthand reports are true. As the apostle John put it: "That . . . which we have heard, which we have seen with our eyes, which we have looked at and our hands have touched . . . [w]e proclaim to you" (see 1 John 1:1–3).

I believe *something* (the words and works of Jesus), but I also believe *someone* (those who were eyewitnesses of Jesus' words and works). John concludes his gospel on this note: "Jesus did many other miraculous signs in the presence of his disciples, which are not recorded in this book. *But these are written that you may believe* that Jesus is the Christ, the Son of God" (John 20:30–31, emphasis added). This is biblical faith: believing what John and the other apostles saw and then said about Jesus.

And therein lies the difficulty, because most of us are from Missouri;

you have to *show* us. *Seeing* is believing. Like Thomas, we want to *see* the angry prints of the nails in Jesus' hands; we want to *touch* the terrible wound in His side. We want to see for ourselves (see John 20:24–29). We feel the rebuke of Jesus' words: "Blessed are those who have not seen and yet have believed" (John 20:29). And we hear ourselves say, "Lord, I believe; help my unbelief!" (Mark 9:24 NKJV).

First, let me say that our Lord is not angry with us because we find it hard to believe. He shared our human limitations and struggles when He was made flesh. Jesus himself had moments of uncertainty and doubt and needed His Father's reassurance (see Mark 15:34).

Angry? No. But He does want us to believe, for our faith pleases Him more than anything else we can do. How, then, can we know with complete assurance that what Jesus said and did is true?

By obeying Him. Jesus made this clear: "Whoever has my commands and obeys them, he is the one who loves me. He who loves me will be loved by my Father, and I too will love him and show myself to him." He also said, "My teaching is not my own. It comes from him who sent me. If anyone chooses to do God's will, he will find out whether my teaching comes from God" (Mark 14:21; 7:16–17).

How does Jesus show himself to us (make himself real)? How do we *know* that He is real? *By acting on His word.* In his sermon "Faith, the Proof of the Unseen," George MacDonald said: "I ask you, have you been trying the things not seen? Have you been proving them? This is what God puts in your hands. He says, 'I tell you I Am, you act upon that; for I know that your conscience moves you to it; you act upon that and you will find whether I Am or not, and what I Am.'"

Do you see? Faith in its true sense does not belong to the intellect alone, nor to the intellect first, but to the conscience and to the will. The faithful person says, "I cannot prove that there is a God, but, O God, if you hear me anywhere, help me do your will."

Faith is the turning of the eye to the light; it is the sending of the feet into the path that is required; it is the putting of the hands to the task that the conscience says ought to be done. It is "the proving of things not seen" and of which we cannot, at first, be sure of, said MacDonald. It is putting Jesus' words to the test, doing the very thing that you suppose to be the will of God.

So whatever your uncertainties, act upon what Jesus is asking you to do today. Don't wait for assurance. Just *do* it. Has He asked you to love a difficult and demanding child or spouse, to bear patiently with a painful disability, to be brave in the face of harsh criticism and misunderstanding? Do it! "What saves a man is to take a step. Then another step," C. S. Lewis said.

You will not be able to obey perfectly, of course—that is something only One has been able to do. But if you choose the right thing and try to do it, God will give you all the help you need to carry on. Then, in time (I cannot say how or when) you will "see" and you will "know" for yourself. Then, your whole being will be caught up in the sheer delight of loving and being loved by our Lord.

And this is that for which we were made.

THINGS I CAN'T DO
ANY LONGER

*You are no longer equal to the tasks which once you
undertook with ease. The eye may be dim, the ear dull,
the breath short, the heart faint, the hand unsteady,
and the golden bowl of life almost broken.
And because these things are in contrast with the
long day of usefulness which you once enjoyed,
you are inclined to be despondent; you feel that you are
a burden to others, and that you are in their way.*

—HENRY DURBANVILLE, *The Best Is Yet to Be*

Carolyn will tell you that I'm an impossibly optimistic person who rarely sees the difficulties in life that others see. I awaken most mornings full of lively enthusiasm, an attitude reminiscent of *Mad* magazine's mascot, Alfred E. Neuman: "What, me worry?

Lately, however, when I allow my thoughts to dwell on the fact that I'm well past prime, I find myself somewhat deflated. Yet these pensive moments can be good for the heart, because they make me think long and earnestly about my motives, intentions, enthusiasms, and real interests (Ecclesiastes 7:3).

My melancholy, as I'm beginning to understand it, comes mostly from losses and consequent disappointment, from the realization that certain activities I've always enjoyed must now be curtailed. There are some things—activities from which I formerly derived great satisfaction—that I can no longer enjoy. They're much too difficult for an older man to do. I'm no longer equal to the tasks that once I undertook with ease.

Such brooding only leads to deeper discouragement, however. So I'm learning to ask myself, "Can I be content with these losses, knowing that losses are part of aging and as such are the will of God?"

Dr. Robert Horton, a Bible scholar and teacher, who, in the zenith of his career, could hold congregations spellbound by his eloquence, in his last years struggled from the feeling that he had been set aside. Churches no longer wanted his services, publishers no longer sought his manuscripts, people didn't ask for his counsel.

"A man discovers one day that his mind has lost its old elasticity," he wrote, "that it is no longer equal to the tasks laid upon it; and that those who came after him are being preferred before him. Fretful impatience cannot alter the facts, although it may murder his own peace of mind. *Let him accept them as the will of God for him; then all the bitterness goes.*"

So, with this encouragement I say to myself, "If I accept my lot with a quiet patience, not chafing against it, I will find that it's not without its compensations." Indeed, as Amy Carmichael wrote, "in acceptance lieth peace."

God's will is a soft pillow for my head and a place of peace and comfort for my heart.

> *Thou sweet beloved will of God,*
> *My anchor ground, my fortress hill,*
> *My spirit's silent, fair abode,*
> *In Thee I hide me, and am still.*

Within this place of certain good,
Love evermore expands her wings,
Or nestling in Thy perfect choice,
Abides content with what it brings.

O lightest burden, sweetest yoke ,
It lifts, it bears my happy soul,
It giveth wings to this poor heart;
My freedom is Thy grand control.

Upon God's will I lay me down,
As child upon its mother's breast;
No silken couch, nor softest bed,
Could ever give me such deep rest.

Thy wonderful, grand will, my God,
With triumph now I make it mine;
And faith shall cry a joyous 'Yes'
To every dear command of Thine.

—MADAM GUYON

THE WORK OF
OUR HANDS

*Life is a vapor, but that is long enough
to do the right thing.*

—RICHARD SWENSON

A few years ago Carolyn and I were vacationing in a friend's condo on the Oregon coast. One morning I got up early to take a walk on the beach, access to which was gained by a winding path through thick bushes that overarched and completely enclosed it. The bushes hadn't been trimmed in some time, and they were crowding into the path making it difficult in some places to push through. Even with daylight it was a dark and gloomy place.

At the bottom of the walk there was a gate that was locked to prevent access to the condo from the beach. As I got out my key to unlock the gate, I heard a noise behind me and turned to face a large, bearded unkempt, sinister-looking man bearing down on me through the bushes. He had a sickle in his hand.

I've been told that your entire life passes through your mind at the moment of death, but the only thought that went through my mind was that I had just bought the farm.

As it turned out, however, my "assailant" was merely the gardener making his way down the path to trim the bushes. He was a rather pleasant fellow, and after I realized that he didn't intend to murder me, we had an amiable chat.

As I moved through the gate and out onto the beach, I began to think about the tenuous nature of life. I've already used up most of my allotted time—exceeded my three-score and ten. Life is too uncertain, too fragile, to treat it carelessly. So I frequently ask myself, "Have I left anything behind of significance? Will there be any enduring evidence that I've been here?"

Augustine said, "Do you wish to be great? Then begin by *being*." Enduring greatness stems from what we *are*, not from what we do. Though we may seem to be doing nothing worthwhile, we can be doing everything worthwhile if our lives are being styled by God's wonderful grace. Set aside through sickness or seclusion, we can still be productive. Bedridden or housebound, our holiness can still bear fruit. "Being" is what matters.

The other lasting thing we can do is to touch as many people as possible with God's love through the kindness and compassion we show. "Even in darkness light dawns for the upright, for the gracious and compassionate and righteous man . . . a righteous man will be remembered forever" (Psalm 112:4, 6).

"We are immortal until our work on earth is done," said George Whitefield. I often think of that maxim when I see a friend languishing, bedridden and helpless, burdened with an active mind in a useless body. "Why doesn't God take him home?" I ask.

I'm reminded then that the time of our death is not determined by anyone or anything here on earth—not physicians, not actuarial tables, not the average life span of a human being. That decision is made in the councils of heaven. When we have done all God has in mind for us to do, then and only then will He take us home. As Paul put it, "When David had served God's purpose in his own generation, he fell asleep"—and not one moment before (Acts 13:36).

In the meantime, until God takes us home, there's plenty to do. "As long as it is day, we must do the work of him who sent me," Jesus said. "Night is coming, when no one can work" (John 9:4). Night is coming when we will close our eyes on this world, or our Lord will bring this world to a close. Each day brings one of those two conclusions a little bit closer.

As long as we have the light of day, we must work—not to conquer, acquire, accumulate, and retire, but to make visible the invisible Christ and to touch men and women, boys and girls with His love. If we have done these things, we will have done all we can do and we can rest easy. No matter what else we've done or have not done, we will not have labored in vain.

So "let us run with perseverance the race marked out for us" (Hebrews 12:1).

THE HIGHWAYS
TO ZION

This world is not my home;
I'm just a-passin' through.

—TRADITIONAL SPIRITUAL

Blessed are those . . . who have set their hearts on pilgrimage," writes the psalmist (Psalm 84:5). I'm fond of that verse, 'cause I'm a traveling man, drawn by a picnicker's hankering for "a better place," and I suspect you may be too.

We wend our way through this world, sampling its pleasures, but we can never settle down. We find our place, or so we think, but then our feet get to itching, or maybe it's our hearts, for as the poet tells us, it's in our hearts that we long to go on pilgrimage.

It's not that we find what we're longing for by looking into our hearts, as some would have us believe, but that our hearts may lead us to our final destination if we listen to what they have to say. If we pay attention, we'll hear them murmur their discontent with this world and their desire for a better place.

And, believe me, there is a better place: our Father's house. Though we may not know it, our soul "yearns, even faints, for the courts of the LORD." We "cry out for the living God" (Psalm 84:2). We're mostly homesick, yearning for our Father and our eternal home. Everything else leaves an empty void.

Many years ago a young philosophy student told me about a tutorial in which he and his professor were discussing Thomas Aquinas's proofs for the existence of God. At one point the professor, who was not a Christian, looked wistfully out of the window and murmured, "There must be a God because I miss Him so." It occurs to me thus that we may find God's presence by first noting its absence.

All through our lives God has been drawing us toward His love and away from other affections. The journey begins at birth, continues through adolescence into middle age, and intensifies as we get closer to our eternal home. His wooing is the source of our dissatisfaction on earth and our yearning for that elusive "something more."

He is also our satisfaction. When we come to Him, we find a companion who, unlike others, will never forsake us. He is a strong, wise, and gentle guide to our destination. His presence makes the present journey lighter, less wearing, despite its peril and pain. "Good company in a journey makes the way seem shorter," said Izaac Walton.

Now that I'm getting closer to the end of my journey, I'm thinking more like a transient. I suppose it's natural. I note that Abraham first described himself as a pilgrim when he was buying a burial plot for Sarah (Genesis 23:4). Time and death make you think about such things.

Most of God's elderly children say the same thing: There's no home for us this side of heaven. Like John Bunyan's Pilgrim, once we've caught sight of the Celestial City we can never be content with anything less. We've found our home in God alone. Happiness is trusting in Him (see Psalm 84:12).

"Home is behind, the world ahead," the hobbits sing as they trudge away from the Shire in *The Lord of the Rings*. For us, it's the other way around: "The world is behind, our home ahead." There are no valleys of weeping there, for He will wipe every tear from our eyes. "There will be no more death or mourning or crying or pain," for the world as we know it will have passed away (Revelation 21:4). That makes the present journey lighter, easier on old hearts and knees.

Put another way, it's the hope of going home that keeps me going. I can hardly wait to get there.

SOUR GRAPES

Their sins and lawless acts
I will remember no more.

—HEBREWS 10:17

S ome of us seem saddled with sinful dispositions we've carried with us through the years. No matter what we do, we can't seem to shake them. Studies in the behavioral sciences do suggest that there may be negative psychological traits that are genetically influenced. Some individuals appear to be born with dispositions toward alcoholism, sexual aggression, erratic work habits, and other personality disorders, and may carry those dispositions with them.

The apostle Paul would agree: "Through the disobedience of the one man the many were made sinners" (Romans 5:19). Whether we go back to Adam or some other relative, whether we talk about major perversions or sins we think of as peccadilloes, every one of us has been cursed by an ancestor, handicapped by his wrongdoing, saddled with insecurities and sinful behaviors. Wrongdoing resides in our DNA, without our consent, demanding compliance.

It's common these days to assume that wrongdoing includes only those behaviors that are voluntary and unforced. If it can be shown that some orientation is caused rather than chosen, we render human choice irrelevant and remove that behavior from the realm of moral argument. Our ancestors made us what we have become. Our fathers have eaten sour grapes and our teeth have been set on edge.

"No," the prophet Jeremiah would say. "Whoever eats sour grapes, his *own* teeth will be set on edge" (see Jeremiah 31:29–30, emphasis added). Regardless of the roots of my behavior, I am morally responsible for the wrong that I do.

But here's the good news: *We're not stuck.* The laws of heredity are not the highest laws. There is one higher—the law of God.

It does no good to excuse our sin, or even our inherited predispositions. The only way to rid ourselves of an evil trait is to call it what God calls it—sin—and bring it to Him for His forgiveness. He can then begin to bring about a cure.

No matter what the origin of our sin may be, it is fully forgiven. Our sin may be awful—so shameful we cannot bear to think about it. But I ask you, can any sin be so terrible that it's not included in the atonement Jesus made? John tells us that Jesus' sacrifice was not for our sins alone, but *for the sins of the entire world!* (see 1 John 2:2). Think of the sins committed in the world this past year and add to them the sins of everyone who ever lived in every generation. All those sins have been forgiven. Is yours excluded? No, because the atonement was an *infinite* sacrifice for sin, even sins we inherited from some corrupt, depraved ancestor.

And so we must bring our failed and flawed temperaments to Jesus, even though our choice to do so is nothing more than the end product of a lifetime of failure and our last resort. We may have struggled so long with our compulsions that we've given up, or given in to them. But God does not despair of us, even when we despair of ourselves. He assures us: "I will forgive your iniquity, and your sin I will remember no more" (see Jeremiah 31:34 NASB).

Some of us are difficult cases. Flawed by environment and indulgence, as well as heredity, our personalities resist change. We have "a hard machine to drive," C. S. Lewis would say. Yet God can take the most difficult and damaged life and gradually turn it into good. He does not leave us in ruins. He is watching over us "to build and to plant" (Jeremiah 31:28).

For me that progress has been neither swift nor painless, but chaotic and subject to agonizing delay. I've made no quantum leaps, only tentative steps mingled with many hard falls. It's been a gradual thing, better seen in retrospect than in prospect. Yet for reasons only God knows, some of us may glorify Him for a time through flawed temperaments. We're so damaged that total healing awaits heaven.

If you're one of His children so afflicted, you can be assured of His promise: there will be progress. The God who started His great work in you will "keep at it and bring it to a flourishing finish on the very day Christ Jesus appears" (Philippians 1:6 *The Message*).

HIS STORY

Aslan seems to be at the back of all the stories.

—C. S. LEWIS

In his letter to the Galatians, Paul writes about meeting the apostle Peter for the first time. Paul says he went up to Jerusalem to "get acquainted with" Peter "and stayed with him fifteen days" (see Galatians 1:11–20). Paul's word, here translated "get acquainted," is the Greek word *historeo*, which means "to visit and to learn about someone."

Paul makes it clear that he and Peter did not discuss the gospel on that occasion, for Paul's perception of the good news came through direct revelation from Christ himself, and not from any of His apostles. I can't help but wonder, then, what these two men *did* talk about. We can't be sure, of course, but the text suggests that Paul asked about Peter's "history"—the story of his life.

As we get older, it makes a lot of sense to reflect on our own story and, while we're about it, to look back and recall God's faithfulness, even in the midst of our troubles. It's important to think about our experiences and view them in the light of the whole of life's journey. We may then see that some event that caused us great pain also brought great blessings to us and to others.

As we reflect on the past, we can become aware of "and rely on the love God has for us" (1 John 4:16). We'll see that our history has been a story of that love coming upon us in stages, from birth to the present.

Birth itself is a gift of the Father's love, as was the gift of new birth when we entered fully into God's love. These are but two of the many good things God has given us, sprinkled throughout our years. For all these gifts we can sing in gratitude: "Blessed is the Lord who has shown me the wonders of His love."

Thinking about the past doesn't remove the reality of our sufferings or disappointments, but it can change the way we look at them. Younger people cannot fully understand why we older folks return to the distant past, but such reflection has its place. And when it is done in prayer and thanksgiving, it can be a source of wonderment and deep healing.

I find that sleepless nights are a good time to accumulate those memories. David wrote:

> On my bed I remember you;
> I think of you through the watches of the night.
> Because you [have been] my help.
>
> PSALM 63:6–7

In this way we turn our memories into holy memoirs.

As I write that, I realize that the word "memoirs" has exactly the right sound to it, because it suggests a *written* account of life's accumulated memories. It's good, I think, not only to *tell* our story to others, but to *write it down* for the next generation. And perhaps someday someone will read our story and, by God's grace, make something of themselves that we could not make of ourselves, for those who come behind ought always to go beyond us.

ASLEEP IN JESUS

One short sleep past, we wake eternally,
And death shall be no more; Death, thou shalt die.

—JOHN DONNE

I have a treasured memory of family gatherings with friends when our boys were small. The children would play while the adults talked into the night. Then, weary with play, the children would curl up on a couch, or in a chair, and fall asleep.

When it was time to leave, I would gather them in my arms, carry them to the car, lay them in the back seat, and take them home. When we arrived, I would pick them up again in my arms, take them to their beds, tuck them in, kiss them goodnight, turn out the lights, and close the door. In the morning they would awaken, secure and sheltered, at home.

This has become now, in my latter years, a parable for me of the night on which we "sleep in Jesus," as Paul would say, and awaken in our eternal home—the home that will at last heal the weariness and homesickness that has marked our days. "One short sleep past," poet John Donne wrote, and then "we wake eternally."

Sleep is an ancient metaphor for death. Poets, prophets, philosophers, and playwrights have equated sleep and death. In sleep our eyes are closed, our bodies still, our respiration so slight that we seem not to be breathing at all.

Ancient writers, in fact, referred to sleep as "a little death." The Greek poet Homer referred to sleep and death (*hypnos* and *thanatos*) as "twin brothers." Cicero said there is "nothing so like death as sleep."

While non-Christian writers referred to death as "perpetual sleep" or "everlasting sleep," however, the sacred text speaks of a "sleep" that leads to a great awakening.

The idea of death as mere sleep is alluded to in the Old Testament. Daniel promised that Yahweh will raise up those who sleep in the dust of the earth, and David refers to the same idea when he writes, "in righteousness I will see your face; when I *awake,* I will be satisfied with seeing your likeness" (see Daniel 12:2; Psalm 17:14–15, emphasis added).

The New Testament writers give the symbol its full meaning. When Lazarus died, Jesus said to His disciples, "Our friend Lazarus has fallen *asleep*; but I am going there to wake him up." Sleep was Luke's symbol for the martyrdom of Stephen, who, when he was stoned to death, dropped to his knees and "fell *asleep.*" Paul writes, "Brothers, we do not want you to be ignorant about those who fall *asleep,* or to grieve like the rest of men, who have no hope. We believe that Jesus died and rose again and so we believe that God will bring with Jesus those who have fallen *asleep* in him." And Jesus made this same reference to a grieving couple on the occasion of their little girl's death: "The child is not dead but *asleep*" (John 11:11; Acts 7:60; 1 Thessalonians 4:13–14; Mark 5:39, emphasis added).

Early Christians seized on the symbol of sleep as death. The catacombs in Rome, which were first constructed and used by the early Christians for burial sites, were called *koimeteria* (from which we get our word "cemetery") or "sleeping places," suggesting that the bodies of these believers were merely resting until the resurrection, a belief reflected in numerous inscriptions on sarcophagi: "He/She sleeps in Jesus."

These early Christians could extract the full meaning of the metaphor because they understood that in Christ, death is *exactly* like sleep.

We slumber and awaken soon after. (We're not conscious of time when we fall asleep.) Thus sleep is good and nothing to fear. Death, in fact, is heaven's cure for all of earth's ailments—"good for what ails us," as my mother used to say. Thus there is a fine irony in the disciples' comment to Jesus: "Lord, if he [Lazarus] sleeps, he will get better" (John 11:12).

But what is it that sleeps? Is it the soul? No, the symbol refers to the *body*, not the soul. The soul does not slumber until the resurrection of the body, for in eternity there is neither time nor space. This is why Paul can write with such assurance: "To be absent from the body, and [in the same instant] to be present with the Lord" (2 Corinthians 5:8).

The Greek verb on which the noun "sleep" is based is *koimeo*, which means "to lie down." Correspondingly, the Greek word for resurrection is *anastasis*, which means "to stand up." We "lie down" in the sleep of death and "stand up" in a resurrection to life eternal.

Paul speaks of "sleeping *in Jesus*," as though that's the key to everything. And as it turns out, it is. It's through our Lord's death and resurrection that we are delivered from fear of death, the dread with which Satan has enslaved the world.

There is great fear of dying here on earth, as evidenced by the effort expended to ignore it, avert it, or stave it off as long as possible. Think of all the industries directed to that end. But nothing works very well or for very long. Sooner or later we all perish, and that prospect can worry us a good deal, even those of us who know Jesus.

I was walking in our park some weeks ago and happened on an old fellow making his way around the track. "How's it going?" I asked in greeting. "Well," he replied, "pretty good, I guess. I'm still looking down at the grass." His point, of course, is that looking *down* is better than looking *up* at the grass, or "pushing up daisies," as we say.

The apostle Paul would disagree. He insisted that death was better than life: "For to me, to live is Christ and to die is gain. If I am to go on living in the body, this will mean fruitful labor for me. Yet what shall I choose? I do not know! I am torn between the two: *I desire to depart and be with Christ, which is better by far*" (Philippians 1:21–23, emphasis added).

Paul was certain that death was the best thing for him. He had no fear of what lay ahead. But occasionally even those of us in Christ give way to dread. We may be free from fear of death itself, but the process of dying is another matter entirely. "Heaven is a wonderful place, full of glory and grace," we sing, but the passage to it is fraught with uncertainty. What will our journey to the other side be like?

Some years ago I read a story about an elderly British woman who, though she lived in the Cotswolds near London, had never been to the city. The train she would have to take passed through a long, dark tunnel, and she was afraid to make that passage. One day, however, she was forced by poor health to visit a medical specialist whose office was in the city. The poor soul boarded the train and worried herself into such exhaustion that she fell asleep—and slept through the entire ordeal. When she awoke she found herself undamaged, unharmed in the city of London.

And so it is: we sleep and awaken to eternal life in our Father's house.

This is why, in the end, we have hope for our loved ones. We may grieve for our loss, but we do not grieve "like the rest of men, who have no hope. We believe that Jesus died and rose again and so we believe that *God will bring with Jesus those who have fallen asleep in him*" (1 Thessalonians 4:13, emphasis added). We no more fear their absence than we fear their sleep in the evening because we know they will awaken rested, full of glorious vigor and well-being.

"The Lord gives and the Lord takes away," George MacDonald said, "but the Lord will give *again* better than ever before." We're all getting closer to that great day.

In the book of Deuteronomy we read this simple statement about the death of Moses: "Moses the servant of the Lord died there in Moab, as the Lord had said" (Deuteronomy 34:5). But the Hebrew text reads: "Moses died . . . *with the mouth of the Lord.*" And ancient rabbis translated the phrase: "with the kiss of the Lord." When I read this, I envision God stooping over His children, tucking them in and kissing them goodnight—to awaken in His presence to His love.

John Donne has a wonderful commentary on death as sleep in one of his sonnets. He begins with his oft-quoted phrase:

> *Death be not proud, though some have called thee*
> *Mighty and dreadful, for, thou art not so.*

"Really?" we ask. "Death not dreadful?"

Donne answers that death cannot boast because it cannot kill us. Death is mere "rest and sleepe," and there is great pleasure in sleep because "much more must flow," a place to rest our weary bones.

BOOKWORM

There is no frigate like a book
To take us lands away,
Nor any coursers like a page
Of prancing poetry.
This traverse may the poorest take
Without oppress of toll;
How frugal is the chariot
That bears the human soul.

—EMILY DICKINSON

I've been a bookworm ever since I learned how to read. My two strongest memories as a child are pick-up baseball games at the park and sitting under a gigantic willow tree in our backyard and reading until it was dark. My parents once gave me a set of bookplates that portrayed a smiling worm sticking his head out of an apple, licking his lips and saying, "As for me, give me a book!" Books were my "frigates" that took me lands away.

And I'm still a bookworm. It's almost impossible for me to sit down without picking up something to read. Among my favorite days are Saturdays when Carolyn and I haunt our local library.

Some years ago I read a short story by Argentine writer Jorge Luis Borges entitled "The Library of Babylon," in which he describes a library that contains all the books that were ever written, or will ever be written, with all editions and all possible variations of every volume. Oh, how I'd love to have a library card for such a place!

Carolyn and I *love* books, and we give away or loan out most of our books after we've read them; otherwise our libraries would take up most of the house. The exceptions are those we cherish and want to read again and again.

My reading tastes have always been more eclectic than refined, I suppose. When it comes to books, I read widely—poetry, history, theology, philosophy, mysteries and other who-done-its—although I don't read many contemporary writers (only a few to keep up with my friends). Most of all, I like authors from the past. To read these men and women is to sit in conversation with some of the greatest minds of history.

Reading engages the mind and ignites the imagination. And mental stimulation is important as we age, for our minds, like our muscles, atrophy if we don't use them. Reading can help us keep our mind nimble, flexible, and strong. Certainly there is some cognitive loss as we age, but we can learn and our minds can expand to the end of our lives. George MacDonald wrote in his last years:

> *So, like bees round the flower by which they thrive,*
> *My thoughts are busy with the informing truth,*
> *And as I build, I feed, and grow in youth.*

Above all, I read the Bible. As John Wesley said, "God himself has condescended to teach the way; for this very end he came from heaven. He hath written it down in a book. O give me that book! At any price give me the book of God! I have it; here is knowledge enough for me. Let me be *homo unius libri* [a man of one book]." This is my prayer as well.

I've approached the Bible in a number of ways over the years, and all have served me well at one time or another. My current method is based on a scheme as old as Jeremiah and John: I *eat* it. (I'm indebted to Eugene H. Peterson and his *Eat This Book* for this reminder.)

I take small bites—a verse, a few sentences, or at most a short paragraph. Then I think about that text for a long time. I read and re–read it, a dozen times or more, reflecting on what the Author is saying and, more importantly, what He is saying to *me*. I've found that understanding comes through patient reading and reflection; every text must be brooded over.

Some sayings are hard, so I must think hard and long about their meaning. And if I ponder the Scriptures long enough, I find there's *always* something there.

The next step is prayer, which I suppose is analogous to the enzymes that break down our daily bread. We chew and then we digest.

Folks have asked me if prayer is essential to understand the Bible, and my answer is "Of course," but probably for a different reason than they may think. Almost anyone can understand the *language* of the Bible, given an application of the rules we apply to normal speech. Paul does insist that those without the Spirit cannot understand the things of the Spirit of God (see 1 Corinthians 2:14), but I believe he was referring not to the words of Scripture, but to understanding their implication for life. I have, in the past, had non-Christian professors whose insights into the biblical text were startling. It was the *meaning* of those insights, the *personal* significance of the text, the deep wisdom that touches and changes the heart that eluded them.

It's here that prayer plays a crucial role, and it's here that the Bible is radically different from other books. Prayer cannot help me determine the difference between prose and poetry, between nouns and verbs, or between commands and general observations about life. That understanding comes from thoughtful effort, not free association, intuitive flashes, or special insight. But prayer can lead me to understand the particular truth that I need for *myself*. I believe that's what Paul meant when he presented Timothy with a series of metaphors and insisted that he reflect on them, for the Lord would give insight into each one (see 2 Timothy 2:7). Reflection on the words of Scripture and reliance on the Spirit of God enable me to see what God wants *me* to see.

Prayer is also essential to rid my mind of pride, prejudice, and the preconceptions to which I so doggedly cling. It enables me to hear God's Word with objectivity and susceptibility, so that I can understand what's being said to my self-will, self-indulgence, and self-reliance.

Truth cannot be rationally assimilated; the process by which the Word becomes flesh and touches our heart of hearts is supra-rational—accomplished alone by prayer. It's for that reason that Paul knelt before the Father and prayed that those in Ephesus who read his words might "know" what could not otherwise be known (see Ephesians 3:19).

Finally, what we eat must be integrated into our being. It's not enough to read God's Word and leave it there. We cannot say we know any truth until we've begun to obey it. As someone has said, "To know and not to do is not to know at all."

Jeremy Taylor wrote: "Be sure to meditate so long, till you . . . get some new arguments against a sin, or some new encouragements to virtue; some spiritual strength and advantage, or else some act of prayer to God, or glorification of him." That step, the walk of obedience, is the hardest part. Here's where we need God's help, for we are utterly helpless to help ourselves.

I find encouragement in a story Russian author Leo Tolstoy told about a cobbler, Martin Avdyeeich, who lost his wife and his little child, Kapitoshka, then lost his faith and his desire to live. One day an old peasant came by—a man known for his godliness—and Martin spoke to him about his despair.

"What then is a man to live for?" Avdyeeich asked.

"For God, Martin!" the old man answered.

Avdyeeich then asked: "And how must one live for God?"

"Christ hath shown us the way. Buy the Gospels and read; there you will find out how to live for God."

So Martin bought a New Testament and began to read. "And the more he read, the more clearly he understood what God wanted of him, and how it behooved him to live for God... And he began to measure his own life by these words. And he thought to himself... O Lord, help me!"

This is my beginning: to know that I am a poor creature, utterly incapable of doing what God has asked me to do—and to ask for His help. In this way I read the Bible these days: I ponder it long and I pray, "Lord, help me!"

Obedience flows from God's love. When I know I am loved and cherished by my heavenly Father, I long to be an obedient child. These days, it is the love of Christ that compels me (see 2 Corinthians 5:14).

THE LITTLE BIRDS
OF GOD

*These birds are emblems of those men that shall
Ere long possess the heavens, their all in all.*

—JOHN MILTON

A leper came to Jesus one day, probably to everyone's great surprise, for lepers were banned from polite society (see Luke 5:12–14). Dr. Luke describes the man as "covered with leprosy," so he must have been afflicted with an advanced case of the disease. He was all lesions and stumps, discolored and disfigured, shocking in his ugliness, a gross caricature of what a human being is intended to be.

Leprosy was a death sentence back then. There was no earthly cure. Lepers were required to wear sackcloth and ashes, emblems of mourning. They were "cut off from land of the living."

Of all diseases, leprosy is the only one singled out by the Law and Prophets and associated with sin. Not because leprosy was sinful, or that sin necessarily led to leprosy, but because the disease was considered a symbol of sin—sin come to the surface. If one could see sin, it was thought it would look something like an advanced case of leprosy. Furthermore, the end of leprosy is like the end of sin: death. Lepers were the walking dead: "a sepulcher, a moving grave," wrote John Milton.

This man lingered on the outskirts of the crowd, waiting for an opportunity to approach Jesus—but not too close, lest he offend. And then he made his request: "If you are willing," he said to Jesus, "you can make me clean." This plain request for healing is touching and profound in its simplicity.

Sick and troubled people normally elicited sympathy from others, but not lepers. They were considered repulsive in every way. Nevertheless, Jesus was "moved with compassion." He reached out to this desperate man and *hugged* him. "Hugged" is exactly the right word. "Touched," the word used by most translators, is much too tame.

Did our Lord need to hug this leper? Of course He did! It meant everything in the world to the man. It was what "daughter" was to the woman with the defiling hemorrhage; what "neither do I condemn you" was to the woman caught in adultery. No one else could or would have hugged this shockingly ugly, diseased man. Only Jesus.

Then Jesus spoke the words "Be clean" and "immediately the leprosy left him." And with that simple, healing pronouncement the leper was clothed in healthy flesh.

Jesus then sent the man off to the temple to show himself to the priest and to "offer the sacrifices that Moses commanded for your cleansing," and here's where the story gets even better. If the man obeyed, the priest would have located the proper procedure and would have read these instructions, written there in the Law for more than a thousand years (see Leviticus 14:1–9).

The priest was to go outside the camp to the leper, examine him, and declare him clean. Then he was to take two live birds in hand: one to be sacrificed, its blood poured out into an earthen bowl; the other to be bound into a bundle with a piece of cedar and a sprig of hyssop (an aromatic, sponge-like plant), wrapped together with scarlet string. After the first bird was sacrificed, he was then to dip the living bird in the blood in the vessel until the hyssop was saturated with blood, sprinkle the blood seven times on the one cleansed from leprosy, untie the bird, and set it free.

The first bird represents our Savior, washed and pure, then slain in the earthen vessel of His humanity, His blood poured out to take away our sin and sprinkled on the sinner to denote *eternal* forgiveness. Or as David put it in his memorable phrase, surely thinking of this ancient procedure, "Cleanse me with hyssop, and I will be clean" (Psalm 51:7). Thus we may "draw near to God with a sincere heart in full assurance of faith, having our hearts sprinkled to cleanse us from a guilty conscience and having our bodies washed with pure water" (Hebrews 10:22).

The second bird represents you and me—immobilized and frustrated by our guilt, our hearts beating for freedom like the wings of that frantic little bird, straining against the fetters of guilt and shame that bind us. The little bird was powerless to free itself until it was dipped in the blood of the substitute and set free—free from the entanglements of past failure and guilt, free from sin's power to oppress and subdue, free to fly home to God.

You may remember Richard Bach's *Jonathan Livingstone Seagull*, that strange little book about the earnest seagull that grunted his way up to God. Bach's bird sounded good on paper—people bought the book in more ways than one—but the essential premise was wrong. We cannot take flight from our own soul-sickness. There are too many strings attached.

It is God's birds that show us how to be free. It's the only way to fly.

> *Behold, I fall before thy face;*
> *My only refuge is thy grace:*
> *No outward forms can make me clean*
> *The leprosy lies deep within.*
>
> *No bleeding bird, nor bleeding beast,*
> *Nor hyssop branch, nor sprinkling priest,*

Nor running brook, nor flood, nor sea,
Can wash the dismal stain away.

Jesus, my God, thy blood alone
Hath power sufficient to atone;
Thy blood can make me white as snow
No Jewish types could cleanse me so.

While guilt disturbs and breaks my peace,
Nor flesh nor soul hath rest or ease;
Lord, let me hear thy pard'ning voice,
And make my broken bones rejoice.

—ISAAC WATTS

THERE IS REST

I'm climbin' up the mountain, children;
Ain't got time for to stay.
Ain't nobody gonna turn me 'round,
Gonna make it to the judgment day.

—TRADITIONAL SPIRITUAL

Is it true? Must I keep climbing? Must I "make it" to the judgment day? Is there a rest for my weary efforts? There is, God assures me.

Our Lord entered into rest when He finished the work of creation. He luxuriated in what He had accomplished and "rested" (Genesis 2:2). Every other creation day had a beginning and an end, but not the Sabbath. It is timeless, eternal. It "remains."

The Sabbath, of course, is but a symbol and therefore cannot be our final resting place. Even the rest of Canaan was not the finale, for that was a temporary, earthly rest. But God promised "another" day on which to rest, and so there "remains" a Sabbath for God's children (Hebrews 4:8–9).

Where is that place of rest? Is it in heaven? Or earth? Both, I say. There is a final rest for our worn-out bodies and weary souls on ahead, but there is also rest in the here and now. "We who have believed enter [now] that rest" (Hebrews 4:3). *Today* is the day of rest. "Come to me," Jesus said, "and you will find rest for your souls" (see Matthew 11:28–30).

There is *the rest of salvation*: "It is finished" was His cry. I have nothing to do but believe that my salvation is complete—nothing more. I can rest assured that God will guard my faith to the end. No one can touch me, for I am held in His hands.

There is *the rest of sanctification*: the One who began a good work in us will perfect it until the day of Christ. We can rest in His forgiveness and grace and know that He is at work to bring us to completeness in the end. When we see Him, we'll be just like Him, He assures us.

There is *the rest of ministry and service.* I am God's workmanship, created to do good works that He has prepared in advance for me. He knows the way through my world and the hazards I will encounter there. He knows my heartaches and the obstacles that must be surmounted each day. I can cease from anxious scheming and striving and rest in His sufficiency.

This is not passivity or quietism. God rested from His labors on the seventh day but works today through Providence; Jesus rested in His finished work on the cross but lives to intercede for us.

No, this is not inactivity, but restful effort, relying on the work of God's omniscient, caring Son.

Thus in all things I must make every effort to enter that rest, as J. Danson Smith wrote:

> *In simple faith to rest*
> *that He, who knows and loves, will do the best.*

So, I say, "grow old along with me, the *best* is yet to be."

A *Heart of Wisdom* was just a start. Now enjoy the rest of the book.

Teach Us to Number Our Days

BY DAVID ROPER

Even more insights and encouragement wait for you in the rest of the book—*Teach Us to Number Our Days*—as David Roper takes you to the heart of the question everyone must face: "Is the second half truly the best?" It certainly can be. Roper assures you that you are not winding down, but growing up into a new season of fruitfulness, and in God's economy nothing is wasted.

Calling you to both frank self-reckoning and joy, *Teach Us to Number Our Days* is an uplifting look at the possibilities that lie ahead.

#AHOW-E8917, 288-page hardcover book, **$13.95***

Find all of David Roper's books at ***dhp.org/DavidRoper.aspx***

Also by David Roper...

Psalm 23: The Song of a Passionate Heart

You probably know Psalm 23 by heart, but when was the last time you truly studied the deep spiritual truths of this well-loved portion of Scripture? In the book *Psalm 23: The Song of a Passionate Heart*, author David Roper explains how you can find hope, rest, and contentment

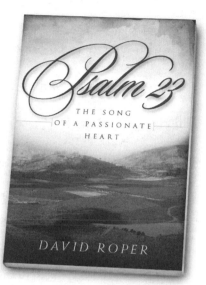

under the watchful eye of the Good Shepherd. You will find real-life applications to thwart feelings of doubt and distrust as Roper walks you through King David's song, verse by verse, helping you explore your own heart and the heart of the True Shepherd.

#AHOW-M7661, 176-page paperback, **$9.95***

DISCOVERY HOUSE
PUBLISHERS®

To order, visit
dhp.org/DavidRoper.aspx
Credit Card Orders Call:
1-800-653-8333

Prices are in US dollars and do not include shipping and processing (call for information). Prices subject to change.

Books by David Roper

A Burden Shared: Encouragement for Leaders

A Man to Match the Mountain: Overcoming the Obstacles of Life

Elijah: A Man Like Us

Growing Slowly Wise: Building a Faith That Works

In Quietness and Confidence: The Making of a Man of God

Jacob: The Fools God Chooses

Out of the Ordinary: God's Hand at Work in Everyday Lives

Psalm 23: The Song of a Passionate Heart

Seasoned with Salt: Lessons from Elisha

Seeing God: Meet God in the Unexpected

Song of a Longing Heart

Teach Us to Number Our Days

The Strength of a Man

Available wherever books are sold. To order online, visit **www.dhp.org**, or call Discovery House Publishers at:
1-800-653-8333